To all of my
wonderful customers~
THANK you!

♥

Judith Ripka

© 2011 Assouline Publishing
601 West 26th Street, 18th floor
New York, NY 10001 USA
Tel.: 212 989 6810 Fax: 212 647 0005
www.assouline.com
ISBN: 978 1 61428 017 0
Front and back cover: Harald Gottschalk
Printed in China.

Foreword by Dr. Joyce F. Brown

JUDITH RIPKA

by Judith

ASSOULINE

A sea of Oasis earrings in 18k yellow gold,
white mother-of-pearl, white sapphires, green jade,
green tourmalines, peridots, black mother-of-pearl,
pink tourmalines, and pink sapphires

Me, wearing 18k gold earrings, a stack of my 18k gold Romance bracelets, an 18k gold ring, a diamond wedding band, and my PN system pearl necklace

"When a woman is wearing my jewelry, I want her to feel as if she is wrapped in one of life's greatest luxuries."

Judith Ripka

Ambrosia Town and Country bracelet, in 18k yellow gold, diamonds, amethysts, mint green quartz, pink tourmalines, champagne quartz, peridots, yellow quartz, tsavorites, and yellow sapphires

CONTENTS

FOREWORD

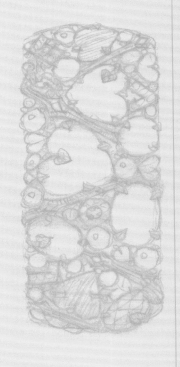

The making of jewelry is an art. The selling of jewelry is a business.

Judith Ripka

Jewelry is about wishes and dreams. And while some may refer to the symbolic value of jewelry in a woman's life, Judith's evolution from a child playing in her mother's jewelry box to a world-renowned designer is the fulfillment of her own lifelong dream. You need only look at her distinctive, elegant, and precision-perfect collections or consider her long record of success as the founder of a now multimillion-dollar international business to recognize the passion, persistence, and sheer determination that started with a dream.

I've told Judith, whom I've known for many years, that she often reminds me of the students I have the privilege of knowing and observing at the Fashion Institute of Technology. Gifted and hardworking, they arrive deeply determined to fulfill dreams they

have been cultivating since early childhood. To them, Judith Ripka is a great symbol. She is that unusual combination of artist and entrepreneur—superb and successful as both. Once they read this book, however, they will also find familiarity and inspiration. They will see in her remarkable story—starting from scratch in her own living room, while raising a family—how she applied the creativity, passion, work ethic, and determination they share to become the eminent master jeweler she is today.

I hope they will also take to heart Judith's lifelong commitment to others. Her belief in giving back has been institutionalized in her company, and causes ranging from culture to health care to impoverished women have been the beneficiaries. Fortunately, education is also her passion. She has created an endowed scholarship fund at FIT for talented jewelry students and has established a formal internship program—one that pays—to help provide that hands-on experience that is so crucial to their education. Indeed, she is also donating a portion of her profits from the sale of this book to the scholarship fund so that even more students can benefit. Judith understands, as well as anyone I know, that success is measured by more than just the bottom line. And in this, I believe she is the ultimate role model for all of us.

Dr. Joyce F. Brown
President of the Fashion Institute of Technology, New York

11

66 My mother taught me to see the beauty in all the little things in the world around us. Each piece of jewelry I design is an expression of that beauty as shared through the eyes of my mother. 99

Judith Ripka

My mother, Fannie

Monaco rings in 18k gold, diamonds, and bold-colored gemstones

66 My first thoughts about jewelry go back to the days when I played with my mother's treasures. She encouraged me to express my individuality and creativity through my designs. 99

Judith Ripka

THE GIFT OF LOVE

I love jewelry. I always have. From the time of my earliest memories, I associated it with happiness, joy, and beauty. My mother was my greatest influence, inspiration, and teacher. She was also my best friend. We did everything together.

My mother was a couturiere, and I would sit with her for hours while she made our clothes. We would discuss design, fabrics, and style. It was her eye that I inherited. While she sewed, I would play with her jewelry, often combining pieces in new configurations and experimenting with them—using a necklace as a belt, placing a bracelet through a belt loop, doubling or tripling a necklace to make it a bracelet. My mother would critique my creations, showing me how to make them even better. While other children played with dolls or games, I accessorized.

Reading fashion magazines with
my friend Ann, 1964

He at sixteen,
babysitting my
niece Lisa

He on the beach in Carmel,
California, 1977

He, 1982

Me, 1967

Every moment with my mother was an adventure. We would take walks around the neighborhood and she would point out the incredible richness of detail her eyes saw—the way a line curved on the pediment on the building across the street; the way the woman walking toward us layered her clothes and used various colors for effect; the way a little boy's face lit up when he saw a big red balloon floating free on an airstream. On our walks, my mother would challenge me to find a new color, shape, or texture and then discuss with me how we could use it in a dress, a coat, or a handbag. My world became a kaleidoscope of shapes, colors, and textures bursting with creative energy and joy. This formed my aesthetic. I knew that I wanted to give to the world what my mother gave to me—beauty, sunshine, and happiness. I wanted to wrap the world in luxury, because I felt we all deserved it. I wanted to make jewelry, and it became my life's ambition.

From a very young age, I had set my mind on designing jewelry. To me, jewelry was about love—the love I had for my family and the love and beauty my mother taught me to see in the world.

"Grey Marilyn (Pictures of Diamond Dust)," 2003, by Vik Muniz. Cibachrome print. From Judith's personal collection. © Vik Muniz/ Licensed by VAGA, New York, NY. Marilyn Monroe was one of my many influences as a young girl.

"I approach jewelry in the same way that many fashion designers approach clothing; It is about building a collection and understanding that fashion is about style and creating a total look, including accessories."

Judith Ripka

A stack of my first bangles with my signature rope-twist texturing, in 18k gold, diamonds, and multicolored gemstones, 1988

66 Some of the lasting impressions of the walks my mother and I would take around our neighborhood when I was a young girl were of the multidimensional details and the structure of the buildings in New York City. My first advertising campaigns, which I titled '18k Architecture,' paid homage to this. 99

Judith Ripka

Vintage collection pieces from my 18k Architecture advertising campaign, in 18k gold, diamonds, and multicolored gemstones

Estate of Mind collection, in 18k white gold, diamonds, sapphires, corundum, and blue quartz

"Judith Ripka's designs in jewelry are unique and extraordinary. She creates with architectural vision."

Dennis Basso

LEARNING MY CRAFT

I attended college part-time while working as an assistant jewelry buyer at the May Department Stores Company for the legendary Dawn Mello, who was later to become the first woman president of Bergdorf Goodman. Dawn was an inspiration to me—a fashionable and brilliant individual who taught me the fundamentals of business. She had the best style, was always impeccably dressed, and, while demanding of her staff, always treated us with respect. She gave meaning to one of my father's often repeated adages: "The harder you work, the luckier you get."

While I was learning about purchases and sales, customer demands, capital, resources, key price points, and top-selling designs, my heart and spirit remained in creating my own jewelry. I saw what I thought was a void in the market and kept designing pieces in my head to fill it. The design part was easy for me: I see the world in shapes and textures, and all of a sudden an idea for a piece of jewelry just evolves from the beauty of a shape or a texture I saw or about which I was thinking.

"Rosie the Riveter (Pictures of Diamond)," 2004, a Chromogenic print by Vik Muniz, hangs in my corporate conference room, a reminder that we can do it! It's created entirely out of diamonds. © Vik Muniz / Licensed by VAGA, New York, NY.

I knew what I wanted to make, but I did not know yet how to make it. Through a friend, I was introduced to a jeweler and model maker. He agreed to mentor me, and in my spare time, between college classes and my work, I became his apprentice and learned to create the very designs I was envisioning in my head. Soon, I started wearing my own designs to work and around town. My friends and neighbors would compliment me on the pieces, and when I told them I had made them for myself, they asked if I could make more of them. Soon I had a little business creating jewelry for my friends and neighbors. I loved that my designs were enabling women to look and feel beautiful.

Then one day I sold one of my designs—a bead necklace—to the Finlay Stores, which operated leased jewelry departments in eight hundred stores. It was my first order! But I needed to make thousands of necklaces to fulfill it, and I couldn't possibly do it alone. So I placed an ad in the local newspaper for someone to help me string the necklaces. A woman who responded to the ad introduced me to dozens of women in her neighborhood who helped me assemble the order. All of a sudden I was in business for myself.

Original bead necklaces with a plique-à-jour Scorpio zodiac sign clip-on, which I created for my sister Rose

Ambrosia earrings, in 18k yellow gold,
diamonds, and multicolored gemstones

“ Judith Ripka's talent has no boundaries. Initially respected as a creative young designer, she is now recognized as one of the most important names in American jewelry. ”

Dawn Mello

Necklaces and pendant from the
Eclipse collection, in 18k yellow gold,
diamonds, and turquoise doublet

Vintage stickpins, in 18k yellow gold and diamonds

❝I always reached for the sun, moon, and stars. I knew I had to follow my passion and try to fulfill my dream of being a jewelry designer.❞

Judith Ripka

" I have always dreamed in color. Today, I gain inspiration from this piece of art. "

Judith Ripka

"Substrat 2 II," 2002, by Thomas Ruff.
Inkjet with Diasec. From Judith's personal collection

“ I have for many years been fascinated with the beauty of Geodes and have collected them for years. Inspired by these natural rock formations, my Oasis collection is my creation of what occurs quite magically in nature. The rich colors and organic shapes give this collection a distinctive modern feel. ”

Judith Ripka

Oasis rings in 18k yellow gold, diamonds, mother-of-pearl, white sapphires, green jade, peridots, green tourmalines, black mother-of-pearl, and pink tourmalines

Oasis rings

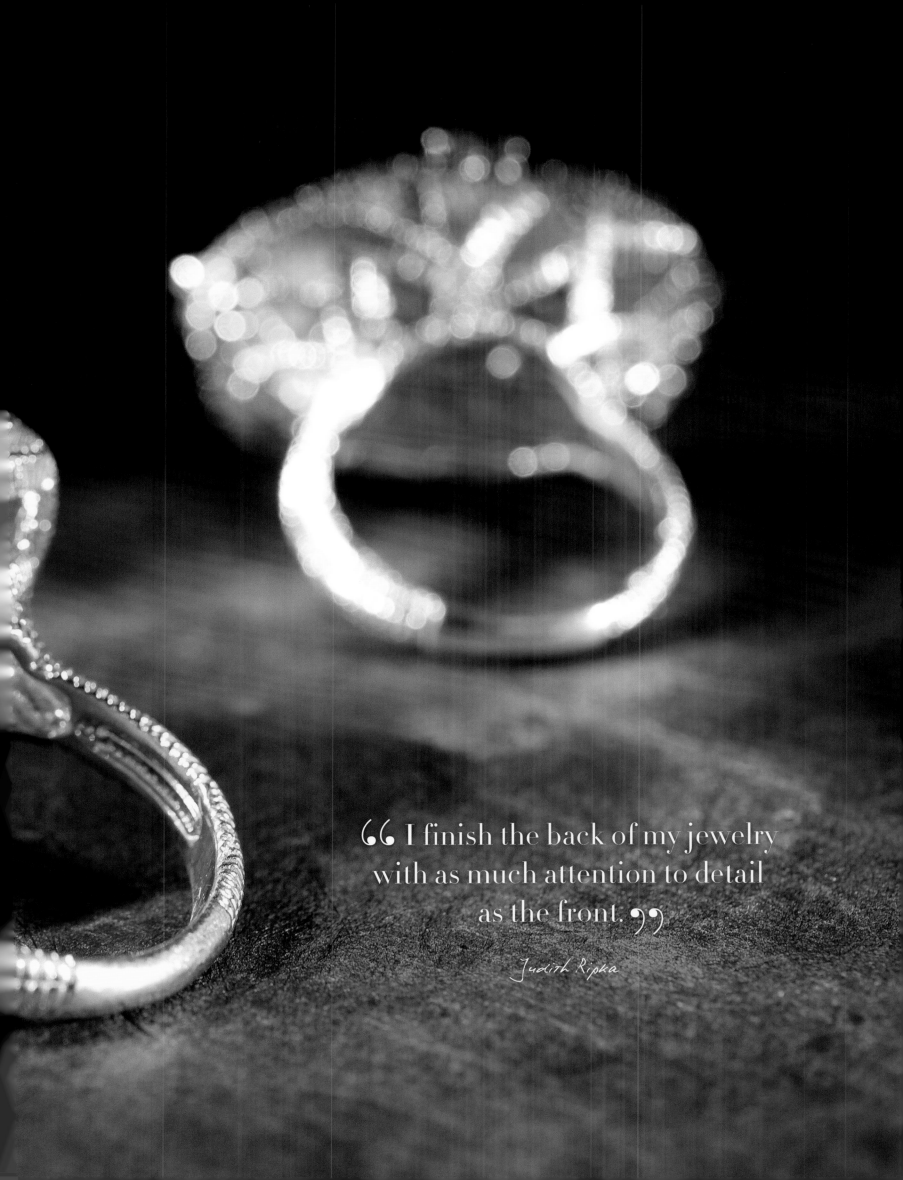

" I finish the back of my jewelry
with as much attention to detail
as the front. "

Judith Ripka

Triple Oasis earrings—one of my most versatile designs—in 18k yellow gold, diamonds, green jade, green tourmalines, and peridots, are wearable for any occasion. Each section is detachable and can be worn single or double for daytime and triple for evening.

" Beyond color, every shape and contour I see shows up in my designs. **"**

Judith Ripka

"Untitled," 2003, by Arturo Herrera. Cut paper on
paper. From Judith's personal collection
Opposite: Cuff from the Dune collection, in 18k yellow
gold and multicolored diamonds

66 Everything around me inspires me—from nature to architecture. As I proceed through each day, I am always attuned to shapes and textures that provide an ample palette from which I draw inspiration. 99

Judith Ripka

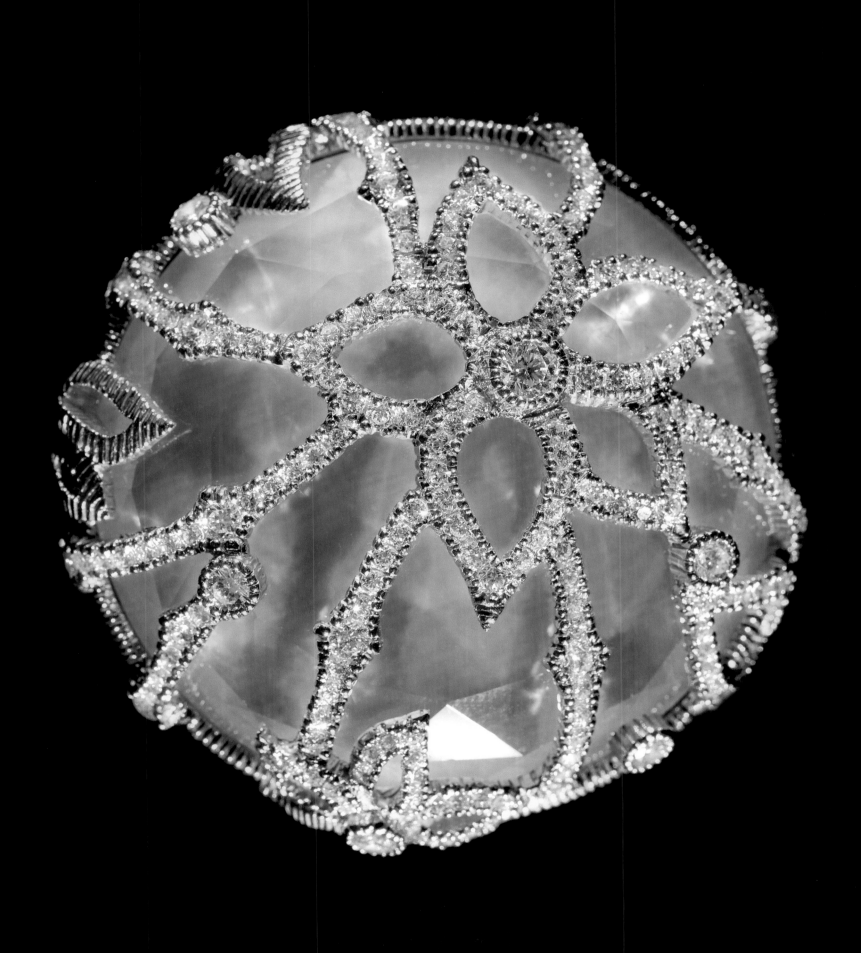

Secret Garden pin, in 18k yellow gold, diamonds, and mother-of-pearl

My Sunlace earrings, in 18k yellow gold and diamonds, were
inspired by winter walks in Central Park.
Opposite: A wintry scene on the Mall in Central Park

I GET BY WITH A LITTLE HELP FROM MY FRIENDS

I now had a fledgling wholesale business selling to department stores. As a wife, mother, and businesswoman, the challenge was to juggle all three roles. While my business was important to me, my family came first. I would make breakfast for my boys and see them off to school, before rushing to New York City to make jewelry. Then I would race home to be there when they returned from school, spend quality time with them, and prepare dinner for the family. Only after they went to bed would I have time to sit down and design. Today they call that multitasking; back then we simply called it Wednesday.

Leaf pin, Heart link bracelet, and multicolored necklaces, in 18k yellow gold, diamonds, and multicolored gemstones, mid-1980s

One day while sitting at my jeweler's bench using a soldering iron
to weld some components together, I smelled an all-too-familiar
odor and looked down to see my long hair on fire. It was the height
of Cher's popularity, and in keeping with the fashion of the day,
I had grown my hair long like hers. That was it—I had had enough.
It was time to find someone to make the jewelry for me so I could
free up my time to concentrate on designing and selling.

I wrangled an introduction to a local Armenian family of fine-
jewelry makers and craftsmen and began a business arrangement
with them that lasted for more than thirty years. They are true
artists and became friends as well. They made the jewelry so much
better than I could, and they gave me an office in their factory
on Forty-sixth Street in Manhattan. Every day I would meet with
them, describe what I wanted or give them a sketch, and then we
would sit in the shop while they fabricated the prototype—often
redesigning the piece as it was being made.

Me with my "Cher" hair, wearing an 18k gold
necklace with rubies, sapphires, and emeralds,
18k gold Alexander the Great coin earrings, and
an 18k gold Alexander the Great coin ring with ruby
and sapphire cabochons. I made the necklace and
ring for myself and then went on to make them for
friends and neighbors who admired them.

Business is about balance between form and function, science and art—and jewelry is no exception. You can design the most beautiful piece, but if it does not lay right or if it cannot be made for the right price, it will not sell. So, as each piece was being made, we would continually tweak it, changing a feature here or there to make it lay right or to reduce the cost without sacrificing the aesthetics of the design. That was the challenge—to find the right balance. Each piece was a true collaboration between artist and technician.

In order to meet my responsibilities to my children, I formed a car pool with friends, and we each took turns picking the kids up from school. Even so, on my day, I often found that I could not leave the factory because of one "crisis" or another and would call my friends to cover for me. They always did. I could not have done it all without them. They were there for me when I needed them. I learned the location of every pay telephone on my way home (cell phones had not yet been invented), so if I were running late and saw that I could not make it on time, I would call one of my friends, who always filled in for me. My friends were my backstop, and they caught me every time I was about to fall.

Monaco rings

❝My greatest creative advice to any designer is to be free and open, and always follow your instinct.❞

Judith Ripka

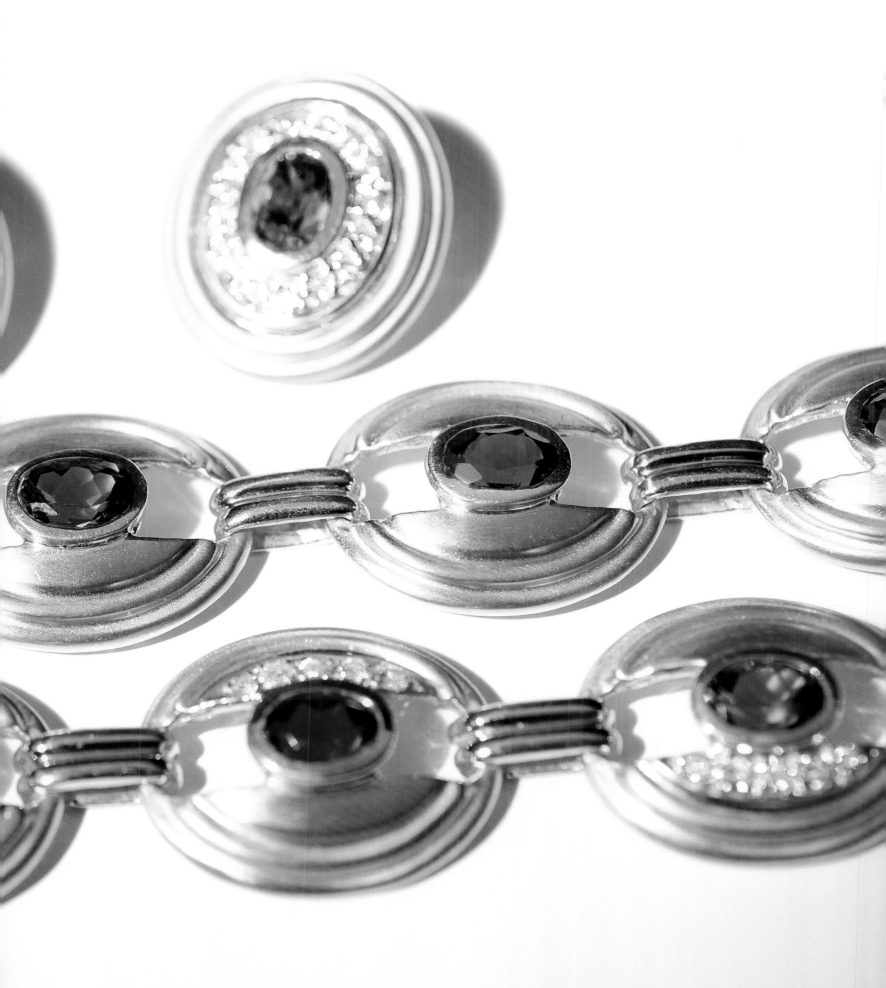

Vintage custom design in 18k yellow gold,
diamonds, and multicolored gemstones, 1983

Vintage custom design, circa 1985.
I created the bracelet in 18k yellow gold with
diamonds, rubies, emerald, and sapphire
cabochons for Ron's mother. The 18k yellow gold
earrings with diamonds and pink tourmaline
cabochons were for his sister-in-law.

IT BECOMES A FAMILY AFFAIR

As a wife and mother, my first responsibility was to take care of my family. Since a wholesale business requires extensive travel to shows and clients, I decided to open a jewelry concession in a local exclusive clothing store owned by two women I knew from my community. That way, if my sons needed me, I could get home in a few minutes.

It was a custom design business. I met with the women who came into the store to buy clothing and would discuss designing one-of-a-kind pieces to accessorize their wardrobes. This was a period of great creativity for me, designing and making special pieces for some of the most stylish women I had ever known. It also gave me the opportunity to create new and exciting pieces every day. I continued this concession until my children left for college.

My best-selling Lola earrings, in 18k yellow gold, diamonds, and canary crystals.

After my second son, David, graduated from college, he came into the business with me. Who knew? Growing up, he appeared more interested in basketball hoops than hoop earrings and in tennis balls than tennis bracelets, but it seemed jewelry was in his DNA after all. He became a certified gemologist and took over buying the gemstones and managing the production and factories, which gave me the freedom to focus on designing. We were a dream team! With this division of labor, we were able to expand the business. It was David who suggested that we reinstitute the wholesale business and start selling jewelry to department stores and independent fine jewelers throughout the country. David spearheaded this division and has grown it internationally, expanding to Dubai, Abu Dhabi, Hong Kong, Moscow, and beyond, so that people all over the world can enjoy my jewelry.

David, in 1971
Opposite: A gem board

64

Without him, the expansion would not have been possible. I have loved working with David for so many years. We share a very special bond, as we pounded the pavement together before the company was a well-known brand. He has always been my right hand, my go-to guy, and I know I can always depend on him.

The best part about working with family is the inherent level of trust. Therefore, when the business started expanding at a very rapid rate, I asked my youngest son, Brian, if he would bring his business and marketing expertise to the company. Brian infused our endeavor with a fresh perspective and an energy that, combined with David's wealth of industry experience and knowledge, has led us into exciting and profitable new ventures. Brian has a dynamic personality and sets the tone for hard work with a smile—he's always the first one in the office at 5:30 a.m. I remember, when the boys were young, I used to tell them, "You can color outside the lines, just not off the page." Brian has carried that sentiment from his childhood to the boardroom, always challenging us to take calculated risks and push the boundaries. He is a true pioneer and has been the first in our industry to envision and execute various groundbreaking marketing programs that have forever changed the landscape of our business.

Brian and me, early '90s
Opposite: Town and Country pin, in 18k yellow gold, diamonds, champagne quartz, yellow beryl, and gold pearl drop

Peter, my eldest son, also sits on our board of directors and has a long-running, successful commercial real estate company. For years, we have relied on Peter to lend us his insight, especially as it relates to retail store expansion. Also a lawyer, Peter has a unique point of view, as he is not involved in the day-to-day operations of our business, though he has the family's best interests at heart. Peter is the son who always puts things in perspective, and to remind me of that, I keep a note on my desk from him that reads, "Dear Mom, Life is good. Love, Peter."

Above: My eldest son, Peter
Opposite: For these custom diamond rings made in the late '70s, I used the clients' existing diamonds to create new designs.

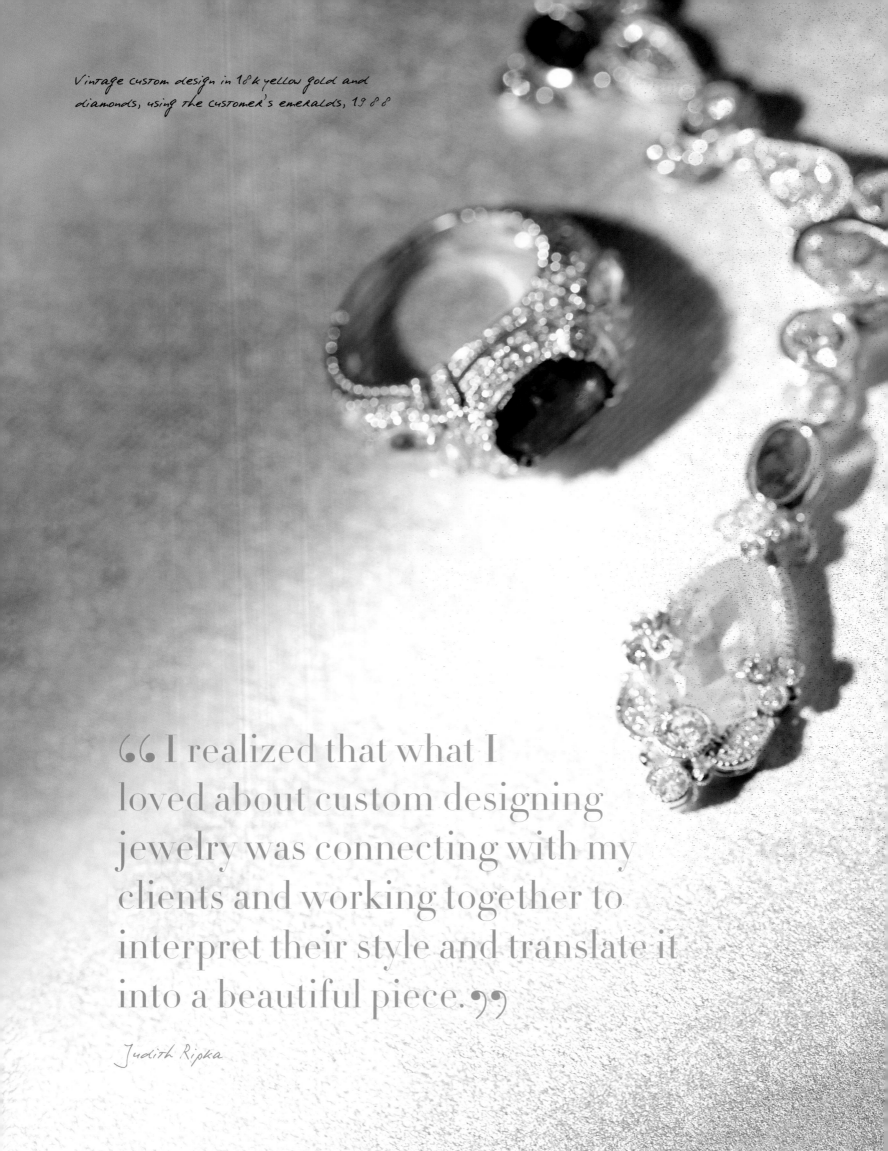

Vintage custom design in 18k yellow gold and
diamonds, using the customer's emeralds, 1988

66 I realized that what I
loved about custom designing
jewelry was connecting with my
clients and working together to
interpret their style and translate it
into a beautiful piece. 99

Judith Ripka

Vintage custom design in 18k yellow gold, diamonds, and pink tourmalines, 1982

"I design for every woman. Adding jewelry to an outfit makes a woman feel like she shines. She feels more glamorous, more beautiful, and more confident."

Judith Ripka

Vintage custom design in 18k yellow gold,
black enamel, and diamonds, 1982.

66 I love every piece of jewelry I have designed. As with my children, I play no favorites among my collections—I love them all! But, if you asked which one I love the most, I would probably give you a different answer every day, depending on my mood and what pieces I was wearing. 99

Judith Ripka

*Estate diamond and black onyx collection in
18k white gold, diamonds, and black onyx*

"The Celadon gold I use in my jewelry is proprietary. Combined with the matte finish—which I championed because of its understated elegance—gives my jewelry a distinctive and recognizable look. It is understated because it does not overpower. In its quiet elegance it allows for its accessory role to augment, not overtake, the sensibility of the wearer."

Judith Ripka

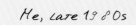
He, 1980

He, late 1980s

He and my sister
Rose, 1987

Ron took me
fly-fishing in
Aspen on the
Roaring Fork
River after
we opened our
Aspen store in
1995

The twins, Nicole and
Alex, all grown-up!

My first grandchildren, twins! It was such a joyous day
to welcome Nicole and Alex, with their proud dad,
my eldest son, Peter

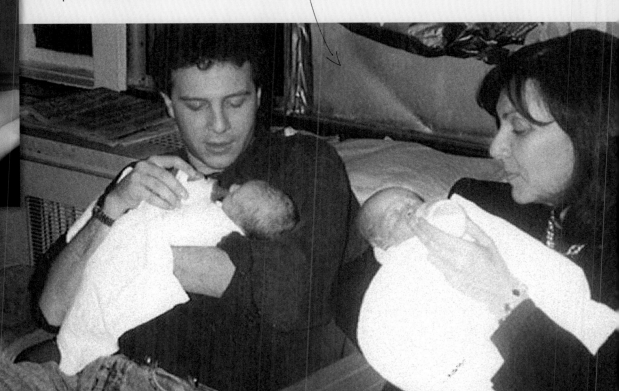

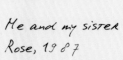

66 The early '80s was an intensely creative time for me.
In 1982, I decided to submit a design to De Beers for
consideration for its annual Diamond Design Award, the most
prestigious of all the jewelry design awards. I created a pair of
men's suspenders, encrusted with diamonds at the points where
they are adjustable and attached to the waistband.
To my amazement, I was awarded the First Prize. Although I am
not known for making men's jewelry, I have made and continue
to design cuff links, stud sets, and wedding bands. I sold the
winning suspenders to Bobby Short, the celebrated cabaret
singer and pianist, who wore them nightly during his many years
of performing at the Carlyle hotel in Manhattan. I also made
another pair and gave them to my husband, who proudly wears
them to this day to all the black-tie events we attend. 99

Judith Ripka

My award-winning suspenders,
in 18k yellow gold, white diamonds,
and black diamonds, 1982.

Cuff links, a stud set, a watch, and rings, in
18k gold, from my men's jewelry collection

Evil eye and horn, in 18k yellow
gold, diamonds, blue diamonds,
sapphires, and white onyx

66 I love Judith's jewelry. It's very unusual how her things can look great with jeans and casual clothes as well as fancy black-tie. Whenever I am wearing one of her long, elegantly detailed chains with several amulets or charms of precious stones and diamonds, I can bet on the fact that someone will ask, 'Where did you get those?' 99

Fern Mallis,
the creator of New York Fashion Week
and an industry consultant

" If I were not a jewelry designer, I would be a sculptor, so I am always interested in incorporating new materials into my designs. One of the most unique materials that I have used was lava from Mount Vesuvius in Italy, for which my husband negotiated the rights to exclusive usage for a period of two years. "

Judith Ripka

Medusa lava pin, in
18 k yellow gold,
diamonds, and lava

Vintage custom designs, in
18k yellow gold, diamonds,
and lava cameos, 1988

"You *have* to wear clothing; you *want* to wear jewelry. When I put on my jewelry each morning, I wear only what feels good. I share that philosophy with the women I design for as well."

Judith Ripka

Berge quilted cuff,
in 18k yellow gold
and diamonds, 2002

66 My favorite expression of my mother's was: 'You can look back, but do not stare.' It reminds me to stay in the solution and not dwell on problems. 99

Judith Ripka

THE LIGHT OF MY LIFE IS THE LIGHT AT THE END OF THE TUNNEL

Beyond being the solid foundation and safety net that allows me to continually reach for the stars, my husband, Ron, is my biggest fan. His enthusiasm and support keep me going, and while the artistic vision is my own, I credit Ron with guiding the business and having the fortitude to help me build a brand. We are partners in life and in business.

In the early days, Ron would stay late at the factory with me so I would not have to be alone. I think the biggest joke between us is when I say: "Just give me five more minutes!" Ron knew better and always came prepared with legal briefs to read, while I worked on jewelry which I had promised to deliver to customers the next day. It was during those late nights that Ron and I would discuss next steps for the business.

Mansfield bracelet, in 18k yellow gold and champagne diamonds

After many long talks, with Ron's support, we opened the first Judith Ripka boutique in Manhasset, Long Island. When the store was complete, we took out our first full-page ad in *The New York Times* announcing the opening. Ron and I believed the jewelry would sell if the people would come.

To continue to build the brand, we started to regularly advertise my collections and market the name Judith Ripka. Lee Solon, the son of my friend Joan, who was later to carve out a very successful career for himself in advertising, came up with the tagline for my jewelry while still in college: "From black-tie to blue jeans and everything in between." It became the slogan in all of our ads. It was firmly rooted in my philosophy that jewelry should be worn every day, for every occasion.

"The Other," 2005, by Matthias Bitzer.
Acrylics on raw canvas. From Judith's personal collection

This concept of designing wearable fine jewelry was relatively new. For years, women had thought of jewelry as an accessory, only to be worn on special occasions. My sales consultants would teach my customers how to have fun with their jewelry, how to mix and match. I became known for my versatility, as well as for creating classic jewelry with a modern twist. To further build my brand identity, I developed a distinctive look incorporating signature design elements and a proprietary formula for the color of the gold, which we named Celadon because of its slightly greenish tint. This shade of gold flatters all skin tones, even making the skin appear to glow. I also started to exclusively use a matte finish because it gives the jewelry a look of understated elegance, so that a woman can wear her jewelry in every role in her life.

66 My life began in earnest when I met Judie. She was everything I could have hoped for in a friend, wife, and partner. I am extremely proud of the way she lives her life—with honor, dignity, compassion, and generosity of spirit. I am prouder even of the business which she has built, against enormous odds, and upon those very principles. I am proudest yet of the family that she has raised, which carries this legacy into the future. 99

Ron

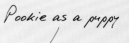
Pookie as a puppy

Ron with Peter, Lisa, and grandchildren skiing in Aspen, 2006

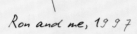
Ron and me, 1997

Ron and me with our five eldest grandchildren, at Brian's wedding, 1996

Ron and me, with our grandson Bradley, 1995

" Judith Ripka's jewelry is unique in character, always up to date and never out-of-date. Judith is an artist and each piece reflects her great design and taste. I receive so many compliments on pieces I've worn during the many years I've been her friend and customer. We are thrilled that Judie is finally publishing this book of her beautiful jewelry for all to enjoy. "

Bonnie Englebardt Lautenberg
and Senator Frank Lautenberg,
of New Jersey

Luxe ring, in 18k yellow gold, white
diamonds, and blackened diamonds

Based on the success of the Long Island store, we decided to take a risk and enter the big time by opening a boutique on Madison Avenue. This was the realization of a lifelong dream for me—to have a store in New York City on the most famous street for luxury shopping. After months of looking, we found the perfect location—a small space at the corner of Sixty-first Street, across the street from Barney's—and we opened our doors in 1995. In 2006, we opened a larger Flagship store on Madison Avenue and Sixty-sixth Street, and today, we have two stores on that iconic shopping thoroughfare.

The '90s were enormous growth years for the Judith Ripka brand. My jewelry was selling, and we were opening more stores—in Beverly Hills, Chicago, Atlanta, San Francisco, Bal Harbor, and Las Vegas.

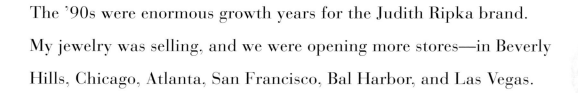

66 My stores are my homes, and I want everyone to feel welcome in them. 99

Judith Ripka

Dallas store, Highland Park Village

Flagship, Madison Avenue, New York City

Sketch of flagship

Bal Harbor store, Miami Beach

Dallas store

Las Vegas store at the Forum Shops, Caesers Palace

Flagship on Madison Avenue and Sixty-sixth Street

66 The wonderful thing about Judith Ripka's lovely jewelry is that you can wear it at any time and anywhere. It's not destined for a dark corner of some safe to be tucked away and forever forgotten. 99

Pamela Fiori,
former editor in chief,
"Town & Country" magazine

"Floating Yellow," 1999, by Erin O'Keefe.
Steel, glass, Plexiglas. From Judith's personal collection

Stack of diamond bracelets and cuffs, in 18k white gold and diamonds

"In the universe of jewelry, the shining star is Judith Ripka."

Cindy Adams

66 My influences date back to the early Etruscan artisans, and from there I continue to draw inspiration from all my predecessors. Estate jewelry that I see at Sotheby's and Christie's has always inspired me as well. I am attracted to the rich history that comes with each piece. 99

Judith Ripka

Stack of my signature Romance bangles, 18k yellow
gold, diamonds, and multicolored gemstones

" Throughout time, jewelry has been
a gift of significance, often marking a
special occasion. To celebrate the love that
accompanies a gift of jewelry, early on
I began incorporating heart detailing into
my designs. Over the years it became one
of my signature design elements, and today
many of my customers fondly refer to me as
the Queen of Hearts. Whether in a boldly
elegant heart-shaped pendant or discreet
heart-carved gallery backs, hearts add the
finishing touch of love. "

Judith Ripka

Lola heart pendants, in 18k gold,
diamonds, and multicolored gemstones.
Opposite: Lola rings.

Chandelier earrings, in 18k gold and diamonds

66 Coco Chanel, Valentino, Giorgio Armani, and Karl Lagerfield have all influenced me. Fine jewelry is after all a fashion accessory. I must know what the clothing designers are introducing, so that I can make jewelry that complements theirs. 99

Judith Ripka

66 Every time I travel to England,
I visit the Crown Jewels, at the Tower
of London, which continue to inspire
me. When Prince William and Kate
Middleton announced their engagement,
I could not help but start sketching what
I believed to be the perfect tiara for her
to wear on such a special day. 99

Judith Ripka

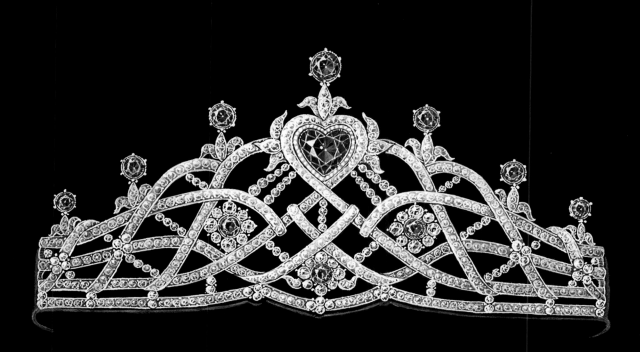

Mansfield bracelets, in 18k yellow gold, white diamonds, and champagne diamonds

Sketch of necklace, pendant, and rings
from my Olivia collection

66 My craftsmen sometimes get frustrated with me because I demand perfection. Something can be a millimeter off, and I want it corrected. 99

Judith Ripka

" My jewelry design reflects my own personal style—classic with a twist. Classically influenced yet modern. In tune with the trend, but not trendy. "

Judith Ripka

Estate deco cuffs, in 18k yellow and white gold with diamonds

PEARLS JUST WANT TO HAVE FUN: THE INCREDIBLE PN SYSTEM

One of my longtime friends, Lee's mother, Joan Solon, came to me with her pearl necklace that she never wore because she felt it was dated and old-fashioned. She asked me to do something with her pearls to freshen them so that she could wear them again. This challenge spurred my creative juices, and I developed what we took to calling the PN—the Pearl Necklace system.

Essentially, I added an 18k gold loop and toggle to the pearls, placed gold sections between each one, and screwed the gold sections and loop and toggle into the pearls so that they could be removed by unscrewing them. This allowed the pearls to be reattached through the use of the same screw in–screw out mechanism, thereby creating five different looks in one piece of jewelry.

Truffle necklaces and pearl drop earrings, in 18k yellow gold, white diamonds, champagne diamonds, bronze pearls, white pearls, champagne pearls, black pearls, and multicolored gemstones

The gold sections could be unscrewed from the pearls, leaving the pearls with just the loop and toggle. Then the gold sections could be screwed together to form an all-gold bracelet, or, if sections were added together, a necklace of varying lengths, depending on the number used. The gold loop and toggle could also be removed so the pearls could be worn in their traditional form. I added diamonds to some of the gold sections so that the PN could be worn more formally, to evening events.

Joan's simple strand of staid, matronly pearls became this dazzling system whereby she could change the look of the necklace to meet the whim of her mood, the need of the occasion—or just to have fun. It could be worn, in the words of her son, from black-tie to blue jeans and everything in between.

Truffle necklaces and pearl drop earrings, in 18k yellow gold, white diamonds, champagne diamonds, bronze pearls, white pearls, champagne pearls, black pearls, and multicolored gemstones

The PN system was a hit. Pearls were fun again! We advertised for women to bring in their pearls so that we could modernize them and make them exciting. In the ads, we used the taglines "Pearls just want to have fun" and "Diamonds are a pearl's best friend." This was the first piece of jewelry for which I became widely known. I sold thousands of the PN system. It became the foundation of my collection, putting my name front and center, as everyone wanted the PN system.

Above, clockwise from top left: All parts of the PN system including detachable centerpieces, bracelet with loop and toggle, pendants, and pins.
Opposite: Joan's PN after I redesigned it, in 18k yellow gold, diamonds, ruby cabochons, and pearls

Versatility and interchangeability became the hallmarks of my line. I started making enhancers, interchangeable centerpieces that could be clipped onto necklaces or pins, so the front piece of the necklace could be plainer for daytime and embellished with diamonds for evening. Creating double-sided hearts—one side matte finished gold, the flip side pavéd with diamonds—added further versatility to the pieces. I redesigned the loop-and-toggle and lobster-claw closures, and added granulation, gemstones, and texture to bring the clasps front and center as a design feature, rather than unnoticed at the back of the neck. This way they could be used as the link from which to hang a heart or other enhancer. These innovations resonated with modern women, who like to mix and match and create their own unique looks.

Pearl necklaces with 18k gold lava pendants

" The Pearl Necklace system that I designed

in 1986, a strand of pearls with a detachable

loop and toggle, was a pivotal piece that laid the foundation

for my collection. It was based on fluidity and a system of

interchangeable components, versatile for wear from day into

evening. The inherent flexibility encouraged clients to embrace

their own creativity and wear my designs in countless ways.

Today, twenty five years later, women tell me that this concept

was a stepping-stone for them to embrace having fun with their

jewelry, as the design can be worn long, short, or doubled, with

or without a detachable clip-on that can be pavé on one side and

matte gold on the other, or as a bracelet—from blue jeans to

black tie and everything in between. "

Judith Ripka

Pearl earrings and
necklaces, in 18k yellow gold,
diamonds, rondelles, and
baroque pearls

Necklaces in 18k yellow gold, diamonds, baroque pearls, and roundelles

Aurora borealis, the northern lights
Opposite: Aurora Borealis cuff in 18k yellow gold,
diamonds, pink opals, pink sapphires, white moonstones,
and hand-cut cabochons

66 Inspired by the aurora borealis, a luminous display of
various forms and colors seen in the night sky, my intention was
to captivate my customers with the same beauty as the heavenly
phenomenon of the northern lights. Most often, the aurora
appears as a diffuse glow and curtains of flickering light.
I was moved by this magnificent display during a trip to northern
Canada, and I sourced stones that resembled the same brilliance,
luster, iridescence, and mystery that I saw in the sky.
My Aurora collection features rare pink opals, pink sapphires,
white moonstones, and hand-cut cabochons that I consciously
placed in a montage to evoke the same magical luminosity
of the aurora light. 99

Judith Ripka

THE POWER OF THE WHITE HOUSE AND THE NATIONAL PRESS

The year 1996 was a very important one for me. I was asked by the White House to submit a design to be considered for the First Lady, Hillary Rodham Clinton, to wear to the inauguration. I created a unique pin engraved with President Clinton's portrait that she could wear on the outside of her coat, over her heart, during the oath of office. It would be seen by everyone in order to signify her love for and pride in her husband.

One of the most exciting and memorable moments of my career was receiving the news from Mrs. Clinton's staff that my design was selected by the First Lady and approved by Oscar de la Renta, the designer of her coat, to be worn at the inauguration!

Opposite: The pin worn by Hillary Rodham Clinton at President Clinton's inauguration, 1997

138

To Judith Ripka with appreciation for your beautiful and meaningful contribution to this historic occasion—
Hillary Rodham Clinton

Hillary sent me this wonderful photograph and a lovely thank-you note. Of course I had it framed.

Ron and me at the White House with President and Mrs. Clinton

The pin was featured in all the newspapers and fashion magazines. Some editors loved it; others did not. The old adage about publicity proved true in this case—it does not matter whether the press is good or bad, just that you are being discussed. This coverage added to my brand identity.

Through the Clintons, I had the good fortune to meet and connect with new, high-profile customers, such as then-Prime Minister Ehud Barak of Israel and Queen Rania of Jordan. Mikhail Gorbachev even got a present for his wife, Raisa, from me. My designs were beginning to be known in the rest of the world. As a result, I was able to open a shop in the Harvey Nichols department stores in Abu Dhabi and Dubai and the TSUM department store in Moscow, as well as see my jewelry carried by Lane Crawford in Hong Kong.

66 In 2010, the U.S. Department of State's Office of Protocol commissioned me to create cuff links for Secretary of State Clinton to give as gifts to foreign dignitaries. 99

Judith Ripka

Flag pin, custom made for a
Washingtonian, in 18k yellow gold,
diamonds, rubies and sapphires,
1997, to wear at the inauguration

Pin, in 18k yellow gold, diamonds,
and rubies with fire opal center stone

"Judith Ripka has a timeless signature style. With each new design, she maintains an element of her core aesthetic while introducing fresh colors, materials, and ideas. I also admire her tremendously as a businesswoman, because of the way in which she has steadily built her business and so carefully expanded her market."

Renée Fleming,
internationally-renowned opera star

TO Q OR NOT TO Q: THAT WAS THE QUESTION

In 1997, a QVC executive came knocking on my door with the proposition that QVC would be a wonderful opportunity for me to further expand my brand and reach new customers.

He suggested that I make a unique and differentiated collection using the same design aesthetics, themes, and looks as in my 18k gold and diamond products but utilizing the less costly sterling silver and semiprecious stones to make the collection more affordable. It would be authentic Judith Ripka, but the price points would be in the hundreds rather than the thousands of dollars. It would make my jewelry, he reasoned, truly accessible for many fans and admirers.

QVC Cocktail ring collection, in sterling silver, Diamonique®, and colored gemstones

The argument was compelling and, once again, Ron was my biggest supporter. As long as the designs were not watered down and were consistent with the integrity of the brand, and as long as the products were made to my standards, it should not hurt the brand, he reasoned. He was right. It turned out to be a great partnership.

As it was when I started my retail business and I was able to interact one-on-one with my customers, QVC has enabled me to connect with the people who call in to my TV shows and tell me what they like and what they want. They e-mail me and contact me through Facebook. And in response to my monthly blog, I receive continual feedback, as they post on the QVC Forum to request specific pieces, critique my products, and make suggestions about how I can improve my offerings to them. I love my customers—their stories, their requests, and the personal touch I get from them. QVC has been a totally rewarding experience in every sense of the word, and I hope to continue to appear on my show until they have to cart me off horizontally!

QVC cuffs, in sterling silver, Diamonique,® and multi-colored gemstones

66 Everyone who has purchased one of Judith's beautiful

pieces knows that she is an extraordinary designer,

one who manages to bring fresh ideas and bold inspirations

to the market year after year. And everyone who has watched

Judith on QVC knows she is a gifted and genuine storyteller.

Those of us (and there are many) who are fortunate to have

Judith for a friend also know that her big talents are matched

by an equally big heart and a generous spirit, and her capacity

to care for her legions of friends and colleagues has no limits.

We at QVC are extraordinarily proud of our association with

Judith. She has played a singular role in building QVC into the

leadership position we enjoy today, and we have been

made better by her friendship. 99

Mike George,
president and CEO, QVC Inc.

QVC bracelets, in sterling silver, Diamonique®, and multicolored gemstones

"In celebration of the centennial of its Gem Gallery in 2010, the National Smithsonian Institution asked me to redesign the setting of the second-largest blue diamond, after the Hope Diamond, in existence. It was also the hundredth anniversary of the cutting of the diamond, having first been cut for Cartier in 1910. The diamond was made into a ring, then sold to Van Cleef & Arpels, who reset it into a necklace and sold it to a South American client. Harry Winston eventually bought it and reset it in a ring for Marjorie Merriweather Post. In the 1950s, she donated it to the Smithsonian. I was invited into the museum's jewelry vault after closing, and I spent hours with the curator and an armed guard as he walked me through the exhibits and showed me the museum's breathtaking collection of gems and jewelry, including a close-up look at the Hope Diamond. We were like kids in a candy store. I found a kindred spirit who could talk for hours with knowledge about stones and designs. It was one of the best times I ever had. Finally, he handed me the blue diamond that was the reason for my visit. He told me that the setting had not been redesigned since the 1950s, and he wanted to see what I could do for it for today's fashion and the modern woman. What an honor! What a challenge!

In addition to designing a new setting, it was decided, with the approval of the Smithsonian, that we would make a replica of the ring with blue topaz in place of the blue diamond and offer it for sale in a limited edition through QVC, with a percentage of the profits donated to the Smithsonian. This ring, with the setting I designed, was introduced to the world through QVC and sold out in less than fifteen minutes. It became known at QVC as Big Blue."

Judith Ripka

The QVC Smithsonian ring, in sterling silver, Diamonique®, blue diamonds, and blue topaz

QVC Diamonique® collection and pearl
necklace, in sterling silver, Diamonique®,
and gray freshwater pearls

THE "O" FACTOR

As big as my brand was growing, its crowning moments were yet to come. While everyone talks about the power of Oprah, it was not fully possible to comprehend her impact until I had the opportunity to feel it personally.

In November 2003, Oprah selected my classic Country Link necklace as one of her Favorite Things and presented it as a gift to her audience. Within moments of the end of the show, my Web site received more than eighty thousand hits and crashed. We received thousands of orders. Quite literally overnight, we acquired a whole new customer base, and an entirely fresh audience was introduced to my designs.

This page: My classic Country Link necklace. Opposite: The Eclipse earrings.

Again, in November 2010, Oprah chose another piece of my jewelry, my Eclipse earrings, to be featured on one of her Ultimate Favorite Things episodes during her final season. It is a huge honor to be chosen once, let alone twice. This time we were prepared—we added server capacity to accommodate the more than one million hits that followed.

My entire office gathered to watch the show in our conference room. I was as giddy as a little girl when Oprah announced to the world that I was one of her favorite jewelry designers. Thank you, Oprah, for everything.

The "Gossip Girl" star Kelly Rutherford, wearing my Eclipse earrings

Ombre earrings, in 18k yellow gold, white diamonds, black diamonds, tsavorites, blue sapphires, blue quartz, amethysts, pink sapphires, black onyx, rubies, yellow sapphires, champagne diamonds, and canary crystal

66 Judith Ripka's signature sparkly designs stand out for their vivid colors and unique textures. They are truly one-of-a-kind statement accessories. 99

Glenda Bailey,
editor in chief, "Harper's Bazaar"

Ombre earrings, in 18k yellow gold, diamonds, and multicolored gemstones

66 From the sparkle to the cut and gem colors to the design, Judith Ripka's jewels always stand out as extraordinary yet not outrageous or over-the-top. Her collections are perfect for any occasion, from day to night, and especially for a glamorous red-carpet look. 99

Natalie Morales,
"Today" show host

Opposite, clockwise from top left: Naomi Watts, Christina Hendricks, Vanessa Williams, Natalie Morales, Suze Orman, Jessica Simpson, Vanessa Hudgens, and Lucy Liu, all wearing pieces from my jewelry collection

" Judith is an incredible designer and a dear friend. Her aesthetic and unique style are breathtaking, and her pieces are elegant and timeless. When I have an important event or just want to feel special, I know that Judith has the right creation for me. "

Kelly Preston

Kelly Preston and John Travolta at the Academy Awards, 2008. Kelly wore my Scallop chandelier earrings, Monaco ring, and two of my 18k gold cuffs.

Above: Garland earrings and cuff, in 18k white gold and diamonds
Opposite: Kate Hudson shimmered in the larger version of the Garland earrings, and Naomi Watts shone in my Catherine earrings on the red carpet.

Above: Snap-lock necklace, in 18k white gold and diamonds, and Estate pendant, in 18k white gold, diamonds, and canary crystal.
Opposite: Angie Harmon, in Judith Ripka earrings, necklace and bracelets during New York Fashion Week, shows how my jewelry can be worn from black-tie to blue jeans and everything in between.

L-O-V-E

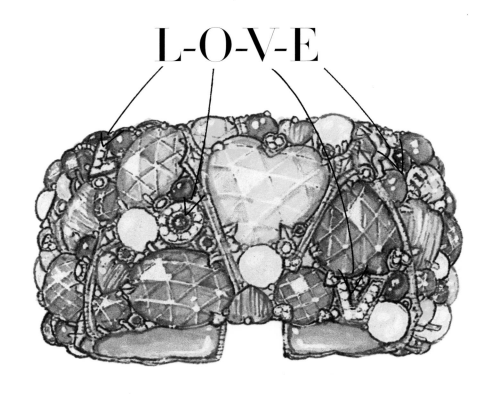

66 If you look closely,
the word L-O-V-E is spelled
out in diamonds. **99**

Judith Ripka

Love cuffs and Ambrosia cuffs, in 18k yellow gold, diamonds, and multicolored gemstones

Love cuff, in 18k yellow gold,
diamonds, and multicolored gemstones

66 I started working with my mother after college, in 1988. It has made us even closer, sharing so many experiences, working through business challenges and overcoming them, and learning from each other. I cherish the time that my mother and I spent together building the company. She has been an exceptional teacher in business and in life. **99**

David Ripka

My three sons, Brian, David, and Peter, 2003

66 Even as a child, I remember thinking that my mom had magic. She made things look better, taste better, feel better, doing everything with style. My mother is a born designer, and it is her innate creativity and flair that has made her a legendary jewelry designer. 99

Peter Ripka

66 My mother leads by example, respecting and celebrating our strengths, so that we all enjoy autonomy in our unique business roles within the company. She always says she wants to create happy jewelry and work in a happy place. We have a great time doing what we do, and we look forward to the next chapter and embarking upon new and exciting ventures. 99

Brian Ripka

" Judith Ripka's jewelry
is not only beautiful
but also very wearable.
I've given pieces to some
of my family, and it is
a delight to see them
wearing her designs
all the time. "

Evelyn Lauder

Vintage custom design, in 18k yellow go

diamonds, pearls, and carved intaglios, 1

Ambrosia bracelet, in 18k yellow gold,
diamonds, and multicolored gemstones

Ambrosia bracelets

I custom designed this necklace for Suzanne Wright, and the bracelet (opposite) was designed as a piece to sell and raise money for Autism Speaks.

" Judith Ripka is a sparkling jewel herself. She designed this one-of-a-kind sapphire-and-diamond pendant for me as a tribute to our Autism Speaks signature puzzle piece pin. Not only has Judith been a wonderful friend to me but she has also been a terrific advocate for the autism community through her other autism-awareness creations. Through our partnership we have been able to shine a spotlight on a disorder that now affects 1 in 110 children, 1 in 70 boys. "

Suzanne Wright,
cofounder of Autism Speaks

66 When I was in Europe
in 2003 sourcing special
gemstones, I found a large block
of smoky topaz which, for fun,
I had carved into a skull.
When I showed it to our
designer of stores, he asked
if I could make it into a bold ring
for him as his signature piece.
Wow, does it turn heads! 99

Judith Ripka

Custom design, in 18k yellow gold, white diamonds,
champagne diamonds, and smoky topaz

66 Judith Ripka is and has been a creative force in the jewelry industry. She has brought great happiness to many loyal followers over the years, and I am certain this will continue far into the future. 99

Burt Tanksy,
chairman of the board, The Neiman Marcus Group

Neiman Marcus One-Hundredth Anniversary Cuff

For Neiman Marcus' one hundreth anniversary, the store selected ten top jewelry designers to create pieces to represent what jewelry would be in the next one hundred years. The challenge for the designers, as established by the Neiman Marcus team, was that we had to use a material that had never been used for jewelry before. It was so unique and challenging in a totally different way. I spent hours upon hours studying materials to utilize—both naturally formed and man-made—as required by the rules of the project. I eventually discovered and selected a geode-like material which looked like bubbles a child blows from soap, which was attached to a backing to form a fabric of sorts. My creation, along with the others, debuted in the Neiman Marcus store in downtown Dallas during a black-tie gala as part of the one-hundredth anniversary celebration.

"One of the best days of my career was having all of my granddaughters join me in a photo shoot for a feature article in the Neiman Marcus magazine, *The Book*, in May 2007."

Judith Ripka

66 Much like her artful and intricate designs, Judith Ripka is an extraordinary and multifaceted woman who has balanced a family and business exquisitely. 99

Karen Katz,
president and CEO, The Neiman Marcus Group

My granddaughters
with me at the
Neiman Marcus photo shoot

Pookie in her jewels

Just me and
Pookie

Aurora pendant and ring, in 18k yellow gold,
diamonds, amethysts, and pink tourmalines

Cushion ring, in 18k yellow gold, diamonds, rubies, and sapphires, with rubellite center stone

66 I feel incredibly lucky to have a full-scale design studio on-site at my corporate office, so that I can collaborate with the jewelers. I think that open dialogue and collaboration is the best way to foster the creative process. The design and production teams share an open work space to support teamwork, ensuring that the jewelry is both aesthetically pleasing and functional. Therefore, every piece of jewelry we create not only looks beautiful but also feels good and lays correctly. 99

Judith Ripka

This page: Estate cuff, in 18k yellow gold and diamonds.
Opposite page: Oasis earrings, in 18k yellow gold,
diamonds, mother-of-pearl, and white sapphires.

" Looking forward to the future, the best is yet to come! I will continue designing new styles, perfecting my craft, and evolving into a total lifestyle brand, which ultimately means designing other products, such as handbags, scarves, sunglasses, and tabletop. "

Judith Ripka

David, my second son, with his wife, Samantha, and three children, Jamie, Bradley, and Katie

Brian, my youngest son, with his wife, Allison, and their children, Jesse and Gabby

Peter, my eldest son, with his wife, Lisa, and three children, Alex, Nicole, and Dani

Truffle necklaces, in 18k yellow gold, white diamonds, champagne diamonds, bronze pearls, white pearls, champagne pearls, black pearls, and multicolored gemstones

ALL IN THE FAMILY

My story is a love story—my love for my family and for my jewelry. When I look back at how and why I made certain decisions throughout my career, what makes me smile is that I created my own destiny and always believed in my dreams.

Today, my chief challenge is to try to maintain the culture of a family business when faced with the growing corporate bureaucracy necessitated by the expansion of the company. Keeping a feeling of family and maintaining a personal connection with each of our employees are two of the things I think we do best, and I owe a big part of that to David and Brian.

I love that my sons work so well together, and as their mother and the founder of the company, it is my greatest joy to see their professional relationships become as strong as their personal ones. I look forward to watching the company's continued growth under their leadership.

And my role will continue to be designing beautiful jewelry for you for decades to come.

With love, respect, and gratitude to all my wonderful and truly loyal customers worldwide,

Judith

Brian and David

Gabby and Jesse in Southampton, Summer 2010

Collecting sea shells in the Hamptons with my grandchildren, 1997

Gabby on the beach in Riviera Maya, Mexico, 2008

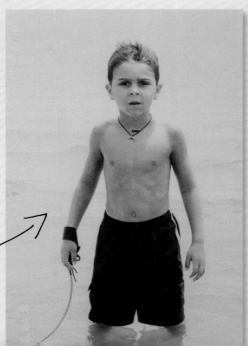

Jamie (above) and Bradley (right), Hilton Head, 1999

Jesse in Palm
Beach, 2010

Jamie, Hilton Head, 2000

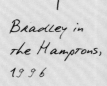

Bradley in
the Hamptons,
1996

Katie in Hilton Head, 2011

THE EVOLUTION

1977   New York City headquarters and manufacturing
facility opens

1982   First leased department in Tango Boutique
opens in Roslyn, New York
Judith honored with De Beers Award for Outstanding
Jewelry Design

1986   Judith designs revolutionary Pearl Necklace (PN) system

1993   First freestanding store opens in Manhasset, New York

1995   New York City store debuts on Madison Avenue
Judith Ripka establishes wholesale division
Aspen, Colorado, store premieres

1996   Judith Ripka creates First Lady Hillary Clinton's
inauguration pin

1997   Chicago store debuts on East Oak Street
QVC show premieres

Romance necklace, in 18k yellow gold and diamonds, 1993

1998   Atlanta, Georgia, store premieres

1999   Boca Raton, Florida, store opens

2000   Beverly Hills store premieres on Rodeo Drive
            San Francisco store opens on Geary Street
            Named one of the Leading Women
            Entrepreneurs of the World by the organization

2001   Judith Ripka silver collection launches

2003   Judith named official jewelry designer, Smashbox
            Fashion Week in Los Angeles
            Judith styled ninth Annual Victoria's Secret runway show
            Necklace chosen as one of Oprah's Favorite Things for
            her holiday gift-giving show

2004   Jewelry chosen for official gift basket,
            Screen Actor's Guild Awards®
            Jewelry chosen for official gift basket,
            76th Annual Academy Awards®
            Judith named official jewelry designer, Olympus
            Fashion Week in New York
            Judith named official jewelry designer,
            Mercedes-Benz Fashion Week in Los Angeles

Signature Olivia earrings, in 18k yellow
gold, diamonds, and colored gemstones

Gothic earrings, in 18k
yellow gold and diamonds

2004	Judith inducted as member of Council of Fashion Designers of America
2005	New flagship opens at 777 Madison Avenue in New York City
2005	Judith honored with prestigious Albert Einstein Spirit of Achievement Award
2005	Bal Harbour store opens in Florida
2006	The Pier Shops at Caesars in Atlantic City opens
2007	Las Vegas store opens
2008	Dallas store opens
2010	Eclipse earrings chosen as one of Oprah's Ultimate Favorite Things for her holiday gift-giving show

ACKNOWLEDGMENTS

There are a number of people I would like to thank for their contributions to my career and this book.

From the very beginning, it has always been about people—the people I have loved, the people from whom I have learned, the people who have helped me in more ways than I can relate, and the people for whom I create jewelry.

My husband, Ron, is my safety net and spirit, and my family is my world. Without them, I would not be where I am today. My three sons, Peter, David, and Brian, along with their wives, Lisa, Samantha, and Allison, and their beautiful children, Alex, Nicole, Dani, Bradley, Jamie, Katie, Gabby, and Jesse, give me pleasure every day of the year. I also want to thank my sisters, Sylvia and Rose, who were my biggest fans, before I even had a business.

I feel lucky to have created a company that has become my extended family. Each member of my team contributes a combination of insight, passion, and loyalty that helps bring my vision to fruition. We have created a unique office environment that is the perfect mix of spirited individualism and corporate structure. There are many who have played key roles in the development and success of my business. Heidi, you remind me of myself, juggling it all. You have been with me for more than sixteen years, always saying yes, while being a super mom to two beautiful little girls. Alice, you have played many roles during your time with the company, handling all with great efficiency and grace. Thank you for helping my voice come to life in every advertisement. Beth, your energy and cheerfulness brighten my day, and your can-do attitude makes everything possible. Linda K., you were one of my very first customers and now are one of my closest friends. That you are now working in the company makes me smile. Thank you for forty years of friendship and always believing in me and my jewelry. Tristan, thank you for designing my beautiful boutiques. Every time I walk into one, it reminds me of just how talented you are. And, to Linda Y., although you retired, we miss you every day, especially your attention to detail, and I thank you for your years of dedication. Thank you to Mark, Tricia, Steve, Rebecca, Matt, Linda B., Irene, Michelle, Steven, Mikki, and Dardana—your tireless hours are much appreciated. More recently, Charles Jayson, who can teach old dogs new tricks, has helped guide us into new business opportunities in this ever-changing world to enable us to become an even better company.

Four people deserve special mention, as they have been with me virtually from the beginning:

Wini Johnson is my alter ego on the design side, who always knew what I wanted even when I could not express it in words. She was the real artist among us, and for almost thirty years, we have sketched together two and a half days a week in my studio, making music and jewelry! From sketch artist to senior artist to vice-president to co-designer and, most important, friend—Wini, you saw it all.

Marie Taranto taught me everything I know about sales, and set sales records that remain unbroken today. I spoke to her at 6:30 every morning for more than a decade, and she told me about the customers who had been in the store the day before, what they looked at, what they liked and wanted, and what Marie thought I should be making for the store. She was always spot-on. When Marie wanted to retire to Florida, I refused to let her leave the company. I opened the Bal Harbour store for her so that she could remain part of the team. She was my connection to the customers and channeled them for me.

Adrienne Rosenberg has been my friend since the fourth grade. When she was married, I was her maid of honor, and when I began my business, she was my first employee. She stood side by side with me behind the counter in my concession in the clothing store and became the manager of my first boutique. While she became a vice president and traveled the country as head of our custom design department, she continued to manage that store until she retired, in 2010. Adrienne—what a ride we had!

Jean Mansingh has been my executive assistant for the past sixteen years. She makes sure that everything and everyone, including me, runs smoothly. Thank you, Jean. You keep it all together!

In addition to my wonderful team, we have been lucky to have equally wonderful partners along the way, including our retailers, many manufacturers and factories around the world, diamond and gemstone dealers, and our partner in producing this book, Assouline. The entire Assouline team has been extraordinary, starting with Prosper and Martine's vision, Esther Kremer's belief in and coordination of the project, Nadine Rubin Nathan and Jihyun Kim's tireless hours and attention to detail, Camille Dubois's creativity, Cécilia Maurin's attention to the images, Mimi Crume's positioning, and, of course, the photographer Harald Gottschalk's distinctive eye, which helped many of these pages come to life.

Last, but certainly not least, I would like to thank Jessica Stark. It was her devotion, dedication, and plain and simple hard work—on top of everything else she was doing, including her day job and raising a terrific little boy—that made the complicated task of creating this book a pleasant experience.

Judith Ripka

Judith Ripka

223

CREDITS